Sally Ride

by Elizabeth Schomel

HOUGHTON MIFFLIN BOSTON

Sally Ride was born in 1951 in Encino, California.

She went to this school.
She learned many things.
Sally loved tennis
and science.

When she grew up,
Sally learned how
to work in space.
She worked very hard.

She went into space.
She was the first
American woman in space.

Sally Ride went
into space again.
She did more work.

Sally Ride got
many awards
for her hard work.

Now Sally talks about
her work in space.